Panda Baby

AT HOME IN THE BAMBOO GROVE

WRITTEN BY SARAH TOAST
ILLUSTRATED BY DEBBIE PINKNEY

Publications International, Ltd.

It is late summer in the steep and rocky mountains of China. In the mist of twilight, Mother Panda stirs.

Mother Panda leaves her den to climb farther down the side of the mountain. She follows long paths and tunnels that connect her den with the feeding places where she will eat bamboo all through the night.

Mother Panda wanders in the cool, damp mist through bamboo thickets sheltered by evergreen trees. She is always looking for good places to eat.

Mother Panda has an extra "thumb" that lets her handle the bamboo leaves, stems, and shoots with great care. Mother Panda spends most of her time eating the tough bamboo.

Panda bears are not able to digest bamboo very well, so they must eat up to sixty pounds of bamboo a day to get the energy they need.

To find this much bamboo, Mother Panda roams over a lot of ground day and night looking for good feeding places. That's why she has several dens and places to sleep.

Mother Panda and her baby will climb down the mountain as winter gets colder. They will not sleep through the winter like some bears do.

Bamboo stays green all year round, so Mother Panda will be able to find plenty to eat during the winter. Mother Panda will continue to nurse Panda Baby for many more months.

Panda Baby is getting bigger and stronger. He goes with his mother on longer walks up and down the side of the mountain and through the dense forest. They wade across streams and swim rivers. They climb trees.

The first snow of winter will soon fall. After a day of playing and exploring, Panda Baby rests in his den.

Panda Baby wakes up to his very first snowfall. He loves the cold snowflakes! Panda Baby wakes Mother Panda and then does a handspring to show his delight.

In the gray dawn, Mother Panda climbs back up the side of the mountain and enters her cave. There she gives birth to her tiny baby. Panda Baby is pink, with only a small amount of fur. His eyes are closed, but he has a loud squeal.

Mother Panda cradles Panda Baby against her chest with her large forepaws.

Mother Panda stays inside the den with her baby. She nurses Panda Baby, but for several days she does not go out to find food for herself.

In only a month, Panda Baby has the same warm fur coat as his mother. Not long after that, his eyes open. From then on, Mother Panda can take her cub out of the den.

Mother Panda will carry Panda Baby everywhere for a long time. Mother Panda can carry her cub using her mouth. She gently picks him up and is very careful to make sure that little Panda Baby won't fall.

It is late in the autumn when Panda Baby learns to stand up. In early winter, Panda Baby is finally able to run and play.

Mother Panda and her Panda Baby roam the bamboo groves to find enough food for the hungry mother. While his mother eats, Panda Baby clowns and plays in the leaves. He isn't old enough to eat bamboo yet.

Mother Panda and her baby search for comfortable places to rest in hollow trees, caves, and other rocky places.